PAST and PRESENT

No 9

FRONT COVER:
STEELE ROAD: Gresley 'K3' 2-6-0 No 61823 drifts downhill through Steele Road station with an Edinburgh–Carlisle freight on 16 May 1959. Steele Road is a small hamlet comprising only a handful of houses. After almost exactly 30 years, the scene on 5 May 1989 has changed little except for the removal of the track, signals and signal box. The station house is in the course of being renovated as a private house and a new access road has been cut into the trackbed. The desolate beauty of the area is very apparent. *Robert Leslie*

BACK COVER:
MUSSELBURGH: Standard Class '2' 'Mogul' No 78048 gets away from the station with a local passenger train for Edinburgh Waverley in the late 1950s. Musselburgh was at the end of a mile-long branch which left the main line at Newhailes Junction. The branch was opened on 16 July 1847 and the station closed on 7 September 1964. In one six-month period during the 1920s, almost half a million fare-paying passengers used Musselburgh station. *I. Swanson*

On 20 May 1990, the railway is but a memory in the town. The location shown is about a half a mile from the former station, the trackbed being used as a road. The terraced houses on the right-hand side survive, as does the older building with the ornamental gables on the left-hand side. A new station called Musselburgh was opened on 3 October 1988, but this is really at Mucklets on the main line, some $^3/_4$ mile from Musselburgh town centre. However, as it is close to an expanding housing development it has been a tremendous success, especially for commuter traffic to Waverley and Haymarket stations.

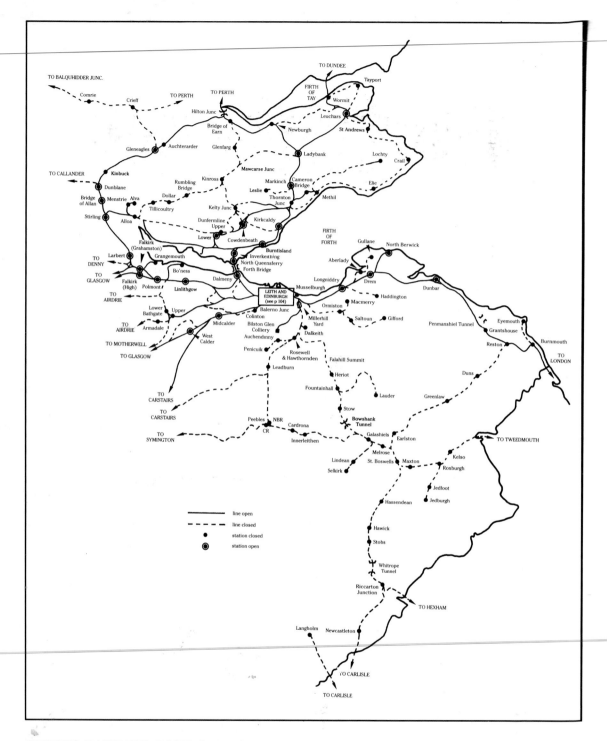

BRITISH RAILWAYS PAST & PRESENT No 9: SOUTH EAST SCOTLAND – This book presents a detailed examination of the changing face of railways in the region depicted in this map. The pictures have been chosen to provide a balanced view, including railways which are still in use or being developed, together with scenes where the lines have been closed and either abandoned or redeveloped since the 'past' pictures were taken.

BRITISH RAILWAYS

PAST and PRESENT

No 9

South East Scotland

Keith Sanders & Douglas Hodgins

On the East Coast Main Line just north of the Border.

Past & Present Publishing Ltd

Note: All the 'present' photographs have been taken by Keith Sanders; the picture credits refer to the photographers of the 'past' views.
All research and captions are by Douglas Hodgins.

First published in 1991
Reprinted 1993
Reprinted 1994
Reprinted 2001

British Library Cataloguing in Publication Data

A catalogue record for this book is available from the British Library

ISBN 1 85895 057 0

Past & Present Publishing Ltd
The Trundle
Ringstead Road
Great Addington
Kettering
Northants
NN14 4BW

2 278557 21

Tel/Fax: 01536 330588
email: sales@nostalgiacollection.com
Website: www.nostalgiacollection.com

Printed and bound in Great Britain

To Gillian and Ashley

DUNFERMLINE LOWER 'J38' 0-6-0 No 65930 approaches Dunfermline Lower station from the west with a weedkilling train on 30 March 1964. The train consists of old locomotive tenders which was the normal make-up of this train in the 1960s. *Rodney Lissenden*

Despite the passage of 26 years, the fence still retains its crooked appearance. The land on the right has been built up and forms part of an estate of luxury homes. The track has been upgraded to long welded rail on concrete sleepers.

CONTENTS

BIBLIOGRAPHY

A Regional History of the Railways of Great Britain
    Volume 6 - Scotland; The Lowlands & the Borders *by John Thomas (David & Charles)*
    Volume 15 - North of Scotland *by John Thomas & David Turnock (David & Charles)*
Forgotten Railways - Scotland *by John Thomas (David & Charles)*

BR Steam Motive Power Depots - Scottish Region *by Paul Bolger (Ian Allan Ltd)*
The Waverley Route *by Neil Caplan (Ian Allan Ltd)*
Encyclopaedia of British Railway Companies *by Christopher Awdry (Patrick Stephens Limited)*
Jowett's Railway Atlas of Great Britain & Ireland *by Alan Jowett (Patrick Stephens Limited)*

LAMBERTON: LNER 'A3' 'Pacific' No 60080 *Dick Turpin* heads north over the Border with a goods train on 13 August 1959. The loco was one of the class still running with a single chimney at this time. The location is 4 miles north of Berwick-upon-Tweed. *J. C. Beckett*

The location, which is close to the windswept North Sea Coast, has changed little over the years. The main changes in evidence on 5 May 1989 are the overhead wires and the modern motive power in the shape of an HST. The attractive Border sign presides over this section of track but is often missed by travellers as trains pass it at such high speed.

INTRODUCTION

In common with most areas of Britain, the railways of South East Scotland have seen much change over the last 30 years, with some lines being upgraded and incorporating all the latest technological innovations whilst others have been completely eradicated. A study of the accompanying map will show that the area under review was not over-endowed with lines, with very little duplication. Most of the routes were part of the North British Railway with the Caledonian Railway being limited to providing routes from the West to Peebles, Edinburgh and Leith, and Stirling and Perth.

Many of the line closures were as a result of the run-down of the coal industry; Fife, Clackmannan and West Lothian were the main areas to suffer. However, the saddest part of the book must be the Waverley Route. This once proud line, which scaled two summits whilst twisting its way through the Borders, was a lifeline to towns such as Galashiels and Hawick. If the line existed today it would be an ideal candidate for treatment similar to that given to the Settle–Carlisle line. There has been very little development on the Waverley Route trackbed and mile upon mile remains just as it was when the track was lifted – even the ballast is still there. The only trackbed developments have been in the towns such as the Leisure Centre in Hawick or a new section of road in Galashiels.

The former Caledonian Railway line into Edinburgh Princes Street station has also succumbed to the motor vehicle as it is now the Western Approach Road. Elsewhere in Edinburgh and Leith the old trackbeds have been turned into a veritable maze of footpaths and cycle tracks.

Not all the old splendour has disappeared, however, for Stirling is currently a positive oasis with its many fine semaphore signals operated from a manual signal box. Regrettably these cannot really last too much longer.

At the other extreme, the East Coast Main Line is now electrified and 140 mph expresses will soon be the norm. Even in the heady days of the 'A4s' or the 'Deltics', whoever would have imagined scheduled trains between Edinburgh and London taking fewer than 4 hours! At the time of writing the Edinburgh–Carstairs line is being electrified and as a result the overhead wires now pass through Princes Street Gardens. This classic location for railway photography has been altered for ever – how the old order changeth.

Finally, I express my thanks to all the photographers who have allowed me to use their 'Past' photographs (without which there would be no book); to the landowners who readily granted me permission to go on to their land to take the 'Present' pictures; to my co-author for digging out the historical facts; and to anyone else who has assisted me in the production of the book. The overall impression having taken the current pictures is that the Scottish sapling is alive and well, and growing exactly where I needed to stand.

Keith Sanders
Longniddry

East Coast Main Line

RESTON: English Electric Type 4 No D256 heads north through Reston station on 15 July 1951. On the extreme right can be seen the platform for the Duns branch, which closed to passengers on 10 September 1951 but remained open for freight until 7 November 1966. The branch had originally opened on 15 August 1849, laid with double track, but the projected traffic figures never materialised so it was singled as early as 1857, only 8 years after opening. *Gavin W. Morrison*

In the modern picture taken on 4 May 1989 an HST heads north for Edinburgh. All the station platforms have gone but the access line to the former Duns branch still survives as a siding. The up siding also survives, as does the former goods shed in the background.

EYEMOUTH: On Saturday 15 July 1961, 'J39' 0-6-0 No 64917 stands at the platform with a local train for Berwick-upon-Tweed. The 2-mile long branch, which left the main line at Burnmouth, opened in April 1891 and was closed to passenger traffic on 5 February 1962. With the coming of the railway, Eyemouth developed as a holiday resort and an ever-increasing number of passengers came from the Glasgow and Edinburgh areas. *Gavin W. Morrison*

On 5 May 1989, apart from the bench made out of old sleepers, there is no evidence of a railway ever having existed here. The former platform area has been filled in to road level and is now in use as a car park.

NEAR GRANTSHOUSE: This famous sign, 1¹/₂ miles south of Grantshouse, can also be seen from the main A1 road in the background, and has survived unchanged for many years. On 27 August 1978, 'Deltic' No 55022 *Royal Scots Grey* heads south. *Hugh Ballantyne*

On 5 May 1989 an HST forms an up express. Apart from the erection of the overhead line equipment, the scene remains virtually unchanged.

GRANTSHOUSE: 'A4' 'Pacific' No 60027 *Merlin* heads a down special on 15 July 1961, as seen from the footbridge.
Gavin W. Morrison
By 4 May 1989 all signs of the station had been swept away and the bridge over the line completely rebuilt. The house in the top left of the picture remains unaltered, as does, surprisingly, the small brick-built lineside hut. The overhead wires now dominate the scene.

PENMANSHIEL: 'A1' 4-6-2 No 60161 *North British* heads away from Penmanshiel tunnel with the up 'Queen of Scots' on 13 August 1959. The train had been strengthened by three extra vehicles which are next to the engine.
J.C. Beckett

Following the Penmanshiel tunnel disaster of March 1979, the tunnel was abandoned and the track was realigned further west, as was the A1 road. In the present picture, taken on 4 May 1989, the white railings of the bridge which carried the road over the original alignment can just be seen to the right of the left-hand electrification mast. The line re-opened on 20 August 1979.

DUNBAR (1): The yard as seen on 25 May 1962 with 'J36' 0-6-0 No 65344 shunting the daily goods train. The line to Dunbar opened on 22 June 1846. At one time, Dunbar was served by a restaurant car service, 'The Lothian Coast Express', which ran to Edinburgh and Glasgow. The train left Dunbar at 07.55 and returned at 17.42, having departed Glasgow at 15.53. *Michael Mensing*

The yard is now in use as a permanent way depot and has a typically untidy appearance. One siding has been lifted and much of the old 'railway furniture' has been removed. The church in the background lost its roof in a fire on 3 January 1987, but it is being replaced and should be complete by the end of 1991.

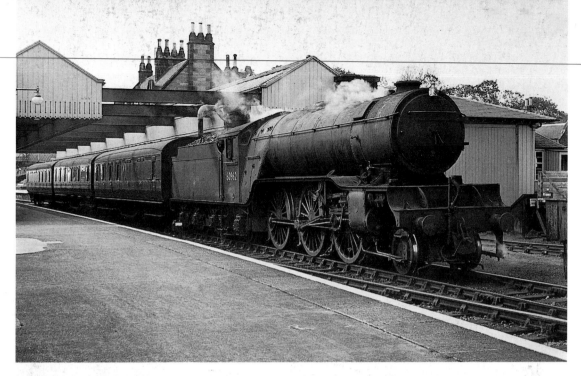

DUNBAR (2): The station stands on a short loop, with the main line passing to the west. On 25 May 1962 'V2' 2-6-2 No 60962 stands in the station with the 15.30 from Edinburgh Waverley to Berwick-upon-Tweed, waiting to be overtaken by the up 'Talisman'. This particular local turn often saw 'Pacifics' employed. *Michael Mensing*

The initial East Coast Main Line electrification did not allow for the existing layout; instead it was intended to demolish the station and relocate it on the main running lines. However, it was discovered that the main station building was listed so the layout had to remain and the loop be wired. The problems did not end there – in order to erect the wires, the roof cross girders had to be removed, and as a result of the ends being burned off, a fire was started which went unnoticed for several hours and caused extensive damage to the ticket office and booking hall. In the picture taken on 3 May 1989, the disused west platform has been demolished and the ends of the girders can be seen above 'Sprinter' unit 150245.

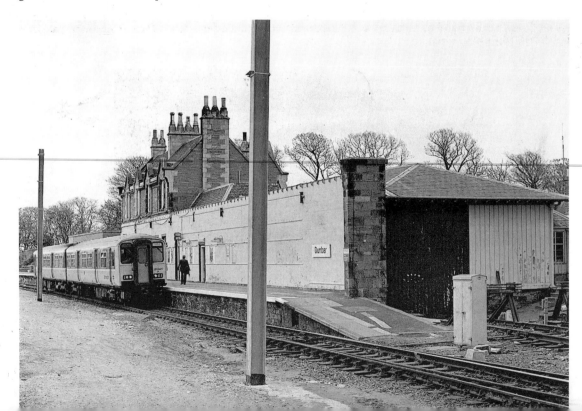

NORTH BERWICK (1): A once familiar scene as 'C16' 4-4-2T No 67492 pulls out of North Berwick yard with the afternoon pick-up goods on 29 August 1956. By this date it was one of the few remaining locomotives of the class still working. Although allocated to St Margaret's (64A), it was, in fact, sub-shedded to North Berwick. The railway came to the town in June 1850 and there was also a station on the branch at Dirleton. Initial results were very discouraging and in 1856 the winter service was operated by a horse-drawn railway carriage. As the town grew so did its popularity as a holiday resort, and traffic on the route rapidly increased. *Gavin W. Morrison*

Today the station bears no resemblance to the earlier scene. The goods yard is now a housing estate, and the station buildings and water tower have been demolished, although the brick base of the water tower can just be seen beyond the platform end.

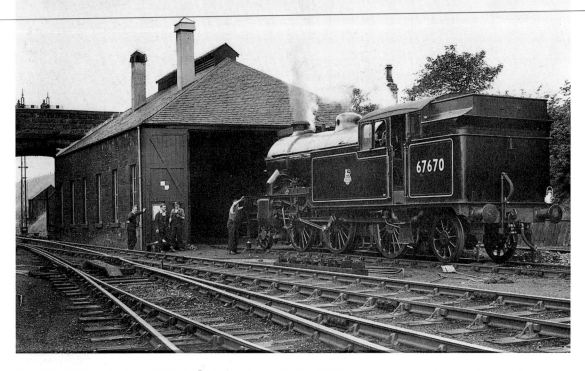

NORTH BERWICK (2): 'V3' 2-6-2T No 67670 receives a final polish before starting its day's duties on 1 September 1956. The shed itself was a rather grand affair, but was seldom host to more than two locomotives. *Gavin W. Morrison*

The present view provides a stark contrast. The track has been rationalised and the shed demolished, but the bridge face does to this day show the mark of where the shed roof was keyed to it. The North Berwick branch is now just a long siding which joins the main line at Drem. No longer do families flock to the town by rail for their holidays – nowadays they come mainly by coach or car.

ABERLADY: The date is June 1964 and the pick-up goods stands at Aberlady station. The branch left the main line at Aberlady Junction, a mile east of Longniddry, and ran through to Gullane, the home of the world-famous Muirfield golf course. It was opened on 1 April 1898. Before and after the First World War, Aberlady was served by a named train, 'The Lothian Coast Express', complete with restaurant car. The Gullane branch lost its passenger service on 12 September 1932, the new buses of the day having stolen the passenger traffic. However, freight traffic continued until 1964. *Norman Turnbull*

The scene on 19 July 1990 shows that although the station buildings have gone, the platform still survives as does the large barn on the right-hand side.

LONGNIDDRY: A busy scene at Longniddry station on 18 September 1967, with DMUs on the up and down main lines and a Clayton Class '17' Bo-Bo diesel standing on the Haddington branch, which joined the main line here. The branch had opened with the North British line from Edinburgh on 22 June 1846, but it was singled some ten years later in October 1856. A siding to the east of the station was used to store a number of Class 'D11/2' 4-4-0s prior to their being sent for scrapping, and many enthusiasts made their way to Longniddry to see them. In December 1953, 'A2' 'Pacific' No 60530 *Sayajirao* was derailed and finished up lying on its side in the main road alongside the station. *Norman Turnbull*

DMUs still feature today on the Edinburgh–North Berwick services although 'Sprinters' are becoming more common, and Metro-Cammell set No 101318 is seen on such a service on the evening of 18 July 1990. The Haddington branch closed on 1 April 1968, and the former island platform has been narrowed. In fact, both the platforms are now some 50 yards further east, as is the new footbridge. The station buildings, signal box and sidings have all gone. The overhead wires were energised on 3 September 1990.

ORMISTON: The station as it was in May 1965, just a few days before closure, as an Ivatt Class '2' 'Mogul' pauses with the freight for Saltoun. Ormiston was on the branch which ran from Monktonhall Junction on the East Coast Main Line to Macmerry. A further section from Ormiston via Saltoun to Gifford opened in 1901. The section beyond Saltoun was closed in 1960 as a result of the bridge over Humbie Burn being declared unsafe. *Norman Turnbull*

The present scene was taken to the left of the older picture because of a large tree now occupying the space! The former trackbed is now a Nature Trail marked out by old signal posts, and whilst the cottage has been demolished, the resulting gap does reveal the loading platform in the former goods yard.

SALTOUN: Ivatt Class '2' 2-6-0 No 46462 is about to depart with the daily pick-up goods in April 1964. Saltoun became the end of the line on 2 May 1960 when the section to Gifford was closed (see page 19). The regular traffic on the line was coal and malt for the nearby Glenkinchie Distillery, with the return traffic being crates of whisky. Seasonal traffic included livestock and farm produce. A large maltings was built at Pencaitland to utilise the railway, but it had not been built long when the whole branch closed in May 1965. *Norman Turnbull*

Despite the passage of 25 years, the small station building still stands, albeit in a somewhat dilapidated condition. The platform face can also be just seen.

The station building and timber-faced platform four months after closure. Surely a perfect subject for railway modellers. *Norman Turnbull*

Waverley Route 1: Newcastleton – St Boswells and branches

NEWCASTLETON: An original two-car Derby Lightweight DMU arrives at Newcastleton station with the 18.13 Carlisle to Hawick service on 28 June 1968. For northbound trains, Newcastleton was the start of a long 10-mile climb, much of it at 1 in 75, to Whitrope summit. Newcastleton was also the scene of a last, futile attempt to prevent the closure of the Waverley Route. When the last scheduled up train reached the station in the early hours of 6 January 1969, the driver found the level crossing gates closed against him and firmly padlocked. Not only that, but it seemed that the whole of the village had turned out at that early hour and they were standing behind the gates further barring the train's progress. They halted the passage of the train for over an hour before allowing it to proceed. Later that same morning, the last northbound train passed through the station. It was a railtour special from Leeds to Edinburgh, hauled by 'Deltic' No D9007 *Pinza*. *Michael Mensing*

All signs of the station have been swept away in this 1990 view, leaving only the station house, which is still in use as a private residence.

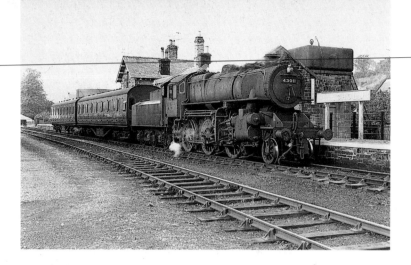

LANGHOLM: The station as seen on 10 October 1963 with Ivatt Class '4' 2-6-0 No 43011 at the head of the 15.28 train to Carlisle. Langholm was at the end of a branch which ran for 7 miles north from Riddings Junction. There were two other stations on the line, Gilnockie and Canonbie. The branch finally closed on 18 September 1967, having originally opened on 18 April 1864. *Hugh Ballantyne*

By 23 April 1990, all trace of the railway had gone and the only recognisable feature is the roof of the house on the extreme right-hand side of the picture. The area is used as a car park for the local authority houses and flats on the perimeter of the former station site. Although the station has gone, it is not forgotten; a stone cairn at the far end of the car park commemorates the departure of the last passenger train on 13 June 1964.

SANDHOLM VIADUCT: 'A2' 'Pacific' No 60528 *Tudor Minstrel* on the 1 in 75 gradient crossing Sandholm viaduct with a special from Manchester to Edinburgh on 23 April 1966. The location was also known as Hermitage viaduct as it spanned the Hermitage Water. *Bob Anderson*

On 23 April 1990, exactly 24 years on, the viaduct itself has been completely demolished leaving only the approach embankments. The northern approach, from where the photograph was taken, is now overgrown with bushes and trees, which the southern approach has escaped for some reason.

RICCARTON JUNCTION: Looking south with a 'Deltic'-hauled railtour in the station. The passengers all look very sombre and no small wonder for the date is 4 January 1969 and the Waverley Route is scheduled to close within a matter of hours of the picture being taken. The locomotive is No 55002 *The King's Own Yorkshire Light Infantry*, and the train a Newcastle–Carlisle–Edinburgh–Berwick–Newcastle excursion.

Riccarton Junction was an isolated location and, indeed, the railway was the only means of access until the Forestry Commission built a rough road from the B6399 in 1963. In addition to the station, complete with public telephone box, there were signal boxes at both the north and south ends and a two-road locomotive shed. The Border Counties line from Hexham joined the Waverley Route here, but the passenger service did not survive beyond 1956 and the line closed completely in 1963. *Trevor J. Gregg*

The picture taken on 23 April 1990 is barely recognisable as Riccarton Junction. All traces of the railway have gone with the exception of the brick building, right of centre, and part of the down platform face. The site at Riccarton was used for dumping ash for many years and now that, in turn, is being excavated. After excavation the ash is barrel-washed to separate out any unburnt coal, and is then screened into different sizes. It is used for making breeze blocks for the building industry, and the recovered coal goes to power stations. In parts of the site the ash beds are over 50 feet thick. The whole of the hillside is now heavily forested.

WHITROPE: 'K3' 2-6-0 No 61854 begins the long descent to Newcastleton with an Edinburgh–Carlisle freight. A 'J36' 0-6-0 had banked the freight up from Hawick and can just be seen to the right of the telegraph pole, at the summit. The date is 26 May 1956. *Robert Leslie*

The view on 5 May 1989 is completely transformed. Whilst the former trackbed is clearly visible, the previously barren hillside is now a vast forest; the fire-break through the centre actually follows the line of Whitrope tunnel. Towards the end of the cutting can be seen the handrails of the bridge where the railway crossed the B6399 road. This bridge is known locally as the 'golden bridge' as it cost a small fortune to build; the reason was the presence of a watercourse under one of the piers which had to be bridged before the main structure could be commenced.

WHITROPE SUMMIT: A classic picture of 'A3' 'Pacific' No 60057 *Ormonde* **hauling a train of red and cream Gresley coaches as it breasts the summit with the 14.33 Edinburgh Waverley to Carlisle Citadel. This summit was 1,006 feet above sea level.** *Robert Leslie*

Apart from the removal of all the railway, the main change is once more the growth of the forest in the intervening 33 years. The foreground cottage has also undergone a few structural changes. The slight gap in the trees on the horizon above the cottage houses a lime kiln, which can just be made out on the earlier picture.

WHITROPE TUNNEL: 'V2' 2-6-2 No 60958 emerges from Whitrope tunnel to complete the last 300 yards to the summit with an Edinburgh–Carlisle freight on 15 April 1961. The 'V2s' were regulars on the Waverley Route for both passenger and freight workings. *Robert Leslie*

The scene is largely the same today except for the absence of the track and the platelayers' hut. It would be a simple job to replace the line here as even the ballast still remains. The tunnel itself was 1,200 yards long and was cut through Sandy Edge; it required special brick buttresses to retain the soft and crumbling rock. The buttresses at the southern end can be seen clearly in both pictures.

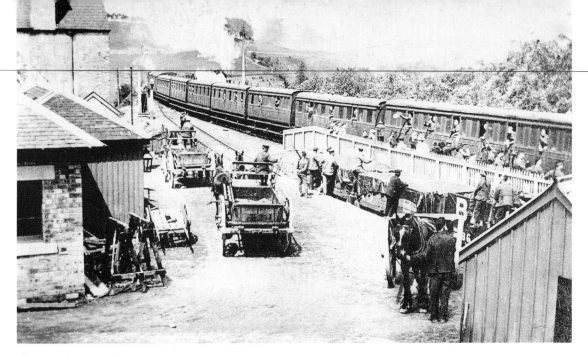

STOBS STATION: A First World War scene at Stobs station with a troop train awaiting departure. There is a complete absence of motor vehicles, only horse-drawn ones being present. There was an army camp at Stobs, hence the traffic. *R.B. McCartney collection*

The ticket office and station house were still intact on 8 April 1990, as were the platforms and (out of sight) the footbridge. The owners of the house are gradually renovating the whole station with a long-term view to restoring it as much as possible to its original appearance. It will be a beautiful home in a picturesque setting when completed. The unusual structure between the platform faces is currently home to a large sow!

NEAR STOBS: A scene so characteristic of the Waverley Route in its heyday. 'V2' 2-6-2 No 60969 of St Margarets shed (64A) pounds up the 1 in 80 gradient towards Stobs with a freight for Carlisle. This area of the line was particularly scenic with rolling fields running down to Slitrig Water. *Robert Leslie*

Barely recognisable as the same location on 8 April 1990, the bridge has been completely removed and the space filled in to provide an access to the trackbed for tractors. The road in the background is part of a circular tour for horse riders from stables at Lynnwood, just south of Hawick. Despite all the changes, a trace of the railway still lingers to this day in the shape of the concrete ballast box in the bottom right of the picture.

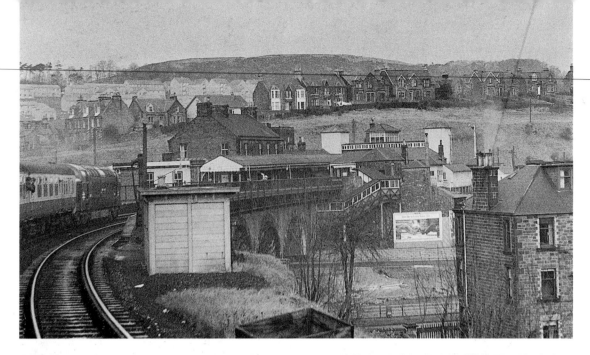

HAWICK (1): A railtour approaches Hawick station on 4 January 1969, headed by 'Deltic' 55002 *The King's Own Yorkshire Light Infantry*. This picture illustrates the tight curve through the station, and the tall signal box can be seen just beyond the station footbridge. The locomotive is just about to run on to the bridge which carried the railway over the River Teviot; the platforms also stretched on to the bridge. *Trevor J. Gregg*

A much transformed picture is seen on 8 April 1990. Gone are the station, signal box, bridge and even the embankment. An exact viewpoint was not possible, but the use of a telephoto lens has reproduced the same background. The site of the former station is now occupied by the Teviotdale Leisure Centre.

HAWICK (2): The station on 12 November 1966 and 'A4' 'Pacific' No 60019 *Bittern* heads 'The Waverley' railtour bound for Edinburgh. The view is looking to the south-west and *Bittern* is faced with restarting the tour off the sharp curve and on a 1 in 150 rising gradient. One of the features of Hawick station was the huge timetable displayed in the station yard. The tracks on the right-hand side led to the goods yard and loco shed. *Gavin W. Morrison*

The modern day scene shows once again the railway swept away, having been replaced by the Teviotdale Leisure Centre and its car park.

NEAR HAWICK: This location is 2 miles out of Hawick, towards Hassendean, and shows once again 'A2' 'Pacific' No 60528 *Tudor Minstrel* working hard on the Manchester to Edinburgh special on 23 April 1966. Hawick can just be seen above the bridge in the background. Note the beautifully manicured cutting sides, probably due to regular, controlled burning. *Bob Anderson*

During the last 24 years, nature has taken over the cutting sides, so much so that it was not possible to take the picture from exactly the same position as the original. The trackbed is currently used as a walkway and is very popular with ramblers. There are plans, albeit rather tentative at the time of writing, to construct and run a narrow gauge line hereabouts.

HASSENDEAN STATION: A rather forlorn sight in January 1970, a year after the line closed to traffic. The station was some 4 miles north of Hawick. *David Easton*

Very little has changed over the intervening 20 years apart from the growth of shrubs and trees. The only items which have gone are the tracks and the pole route. The waiting room, complete with awning, still stands on the down platform although it is hidden from view by the trees. The station is now the responsibility of Buccleuch Estates and they have placed a warning notice on the footbridge indicating that is it unsafe to use.

MAXTON: Standard Class '2' 2-6-0 No 78048 leaves Maxton station on 26 August 1960 with the 14.21 from Kelso to St Boswells. Whilst it has the appearance of double track, there was only a platform on one side in latter years. When it opened in June 1851 the line was double track, but it was singled long before it closed to passengers on 15 June 1964. *Hugh Ballantyne*

The same view on 8 April 1990 reveals that the platform, signals and signal box have all long since gone. One of the level crossing gates remains, as does one of the ornamental gate posts. These items do at least indicate that there once was a railway at this spot. The occupier of the station house is an amateur radio enthusiast, hence the number of radio aerials.

ROXBURGH STATION: A scene of tremendous activity on 9 July 1961 following the arrival of an RCTS special off the Jedburgh branch headed by 'J37' 0-6-0 No 64624 and preserved 'D34' 4-4-0 *Glen Douglas*. Roxburgh was the junction of the Kelso and Jedburgh branches, but it was in a remote location. The line finally closed on 1 April 1968. *Gavin W. Morrison*

The station site as seen on 27 July 1989 is now an organic market garden with crops and fruit trees growing where the trains once ran. The station building, unfortunately not visible in either picture, has been beautifully renovated as a private house.

JEDFOOT STATION: A special tour train returning from Jedburgh arrives at Jedfoot station behind 'B1' 4-6-0 No 61324 on 14 April 1963. The line from Roxburgh to Jedburgh was opened on 17 July 1856 and was known as the Jedburgh Railway. It was taken over by the North British Railway on 3 July 1860. Following severe floods in August 1948, the branch lost its passenger service but it remained open to freight traffic. *Rodney Lissenden*

Amazingly, on 8 April 1990 the platform survives, as does the fence, although the five-barred gate looks a little the worse for wear. Note the amount of erosion of the river bank. As usual nature is slowly reclaiming the area with trees. The bridge in the 'past' picture carried the A698 road over Jed Water and the road then crossed the railway by a level crossing. In 1970 the road was realigned across a new bridge to the south of this location and the old bridge was demolished.

KELSO (1): The scene at Kelso station on 18 July 1962, with Standard Class '2' 2-6-0 No 78047 standing in the bay platform with a local train to Berwick-upon-Tweed. The railway came to the outskirts of Kelso in June 1850 and one year later reached the town proper. For a period trains ran from Edinburgh to Berwick via Galashiels and Kelso. The line closed to passengers on 15 June 1964 and four years later, on 1 April 1968, it closed to freight.
Noel A. Machell

By 27 July 1989 there had been a vast change. Only the roadbridge and the long building on the right remain. The trackbed has been filled in to platform height and the site is now part of a plastics factory.

KELSO (2): Standard Class '2' 'Mogul' No 78048 works the 16.00 St Boswells to Berwick-upon-Tweed local service on 26 May 1962. The train consists of one coach only, a scene which was once so familiar but is now just a memory. *Michael Mensing*

The bridge and the long building are all that really link the two pictures, although part of the platform edging can just by discerned on the extreme left. The station yard is now occupied by a Lada dealership – hardly a fair exchange!

KELSO (3): The 16.00 St Boswells to Berwick-upon-Tweed has been propelled into the bay platform in order to attach parcels vans to its single coach. Standard Class '2' No 78047 is in charge on 30 May 1962. *Michael Mensing*

All the railway has been removed, or has it? Just behind and to the left of the cement mixer can be seen part of the bay platform edging where the coach is standing in the 'past' picture. Everything else has been surrendered to local industry.

ST BOSWELLS (1): On 26 May 1962, Standard Class '2' No 78049 is about to couple up to its coach in the down platform after running around. It will then cross over to the up platform. To the south of the station was Kelso Junction where the line to Kelso and Jedburgh diverged, whilst 1 mile to the north was Ravenswood Junction where the Earlston line left the Waverley Route. In 1920, something of a boom year for the railway in these parts, over half a million sheep and cattle were transported by rail from St Boswells. There was a signal box at either end of the station and even a two-road engine shed. *Michael Mensing*

Today all trace of this part of the station has gone. The modern building on the left-hand side is the headquarters of the Borders Regional Council.

ST BOSWELLS (2): BR/Sulzer 1Co-Co1 diesel-electric No D13 of Leeds Neville Hill depot stands at the head of the 14.36 Edinburgh Waverley to Carlisle train on 26 May 1962. The loco was barely three years old at this time. In the bay platform is the 16.00 to Berwick-upon-Tweed, whilst on the extreme right is the engine shed. *Michael Mensing*

On 8 April 1990 the remains of the platform can still be seen, as can the locomotive shed, which survives intact, although the entrance has been walled up. The shed is now owned by Baxter & Johnston, a company which distributes fuels and oils.

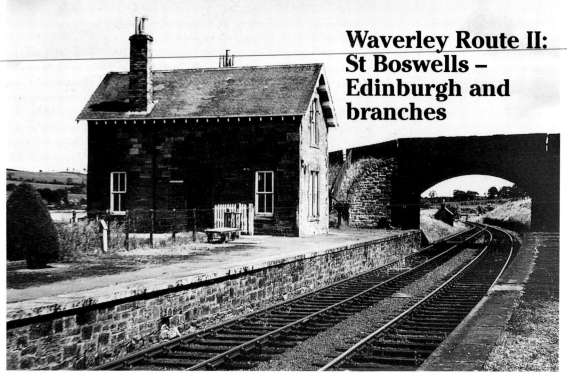

Waverley Route II: St Boswells – Edinburgh and branches

GREENLAW: The station as it was in July 1965. Greenlaw was located on the line from Reston to Earlston via Duns, and lost its passenger service on 12 August 1948 following severe flooding. The line from Reston to Duns closed on 7 November 1966, having lost its passenger service on 10 September 1951. *Norman Turnbull*

By 4 August 1990, very little had changed. The station house, bridge and platforms still remain, although the space between the platform faces has been infilled to form a garden, and the bridge opening has been boarded up with corrugated steel sheets. The house is now a private dwelling, but apart from the neatly manicured bush on the left having run wild, and the removal of a couple of chimney pots, there has not been a lot of change over 25 years.

MELROSE: Looking west on 25 September 1961 as 'A3' 4-6-2 No 60093 *Coronach* runs into the station with the 14.36 Edinburgh Waverley to Carlisle service. Melrose was unusual in that it was one of the few stations on the Waverley Route set on a straight section of track. It was also one of the neatest and best-kept stations on the line, and for many years the flower beds were much admired by travellers. *W.A.C. Smith*

The 'present' scene, taken on 4 August 1990, shows that the trackbed is now part of the Melrose bypass and all the platform buildings and signal box on the down side have been demolished. By way of contrast, the up platform and buildings have survived and, indeed, the building is now listed as being of historical interest. In addition, part of it houses a model railway layout and sells models and books – it is well worth a visit (it was up for sale when the photograph was being taken).

With all those fine chimneys, carved gable ends and attractive platform awning, it is hardly surprising that it is a listed building.

LINDEAN: Lindean and Abbotsford Ferry were the only intermediate stations on the Selkirk branch. Despite being taken on 4 January 1965, only two months after closure, the station has a most run-down appearance. The opening of the branch on 5 April 1856 helped to bring prosperity to Selkirk and in the peak year of 1920, revenue from the branch reached the grand total of £35,000. *Norman Turnbull*

By August 1990 again road has taken over from rail, the trackbed now being part of the realigned A7 trunk road. Motorists would hardly believe that a small station once existed at this spot. In fact, the only item to link the pictures is the cottage on the left which can just be seen behind the platform building in the 'past' picture.

GALASHIELS: 'A3' 'Pacific' No 60093 *Coronach* again, pulling out of the station with the 12.00 Edinburgh Waverley to Carlisle working on 26 August 1960. The locomotive was allocated to Carlisle Canal shed (12C) and was a regular on the Waverley Route. Galashiels was one of the principal stations in the area with traffic from Selkirk and Peebles converging on the town. The line was used extensively by the farming community to move livestock to market, and of course the woollen industry generated a great deal of traffic. There was also an ever-increasing amount of tourist traffic and the peak of the boom in the Tweed towns was in the 1920s; in 1920 alone, 275,000 passenger tickets were purchased at Galashiels station, and goods traffic in the same year brought in roughly the same amount of revenue. *Hugh Ballantyne*

The skew bridge of 'Station Brae' is one of the features of the past scene which remains to this day; it ran across the station above the platform awnings. The former trackbed is now part of a new road and a Health Centre occupies the goods yard site.

BOWSHANK TUNNEL: North from Galashiels the Waverley Route followed the valley of Gala Water which it crossed and re-crossed. At Bowshank, some 4 miles from Galashiels, the line not only crossed the river but also tunnelled through a spur of land. This picture, taken on 26 May 1962, shows the 14.36 from Edinburgh Waverley about to enter the tunnel behind 'Peak' diesel No D13. The tunnel was 249 yards long with a steel lattice bridge at each end. *Michael Mensing*

On 23 July 1989 the bridge is still intact, but the tunnel mouth is totally obscured by a wall of trees.

STOW: A class of locomotive which was no stranger to the Waverley Route – 'V2' 2-6-2 No 60836 heads north past the village of Stow with 'The Granite City' railtour in September 1966. *Les Nixon*

By 23 July 1989 the trees have taken over completely, obscuring both the trackbed and the river beyond. Even the tree by the house on the extreme left of the picture is now higher than the chimney pots. The distinctive shape of the forest on the hillside, however, remains.

HERIOT: Taken at the end of January 1969, nearly a month after closure, the line has all the appearance of an operational railway – only a train is required to complete the picture. Heriot was situated just south of Falahill summit and was one of several stations on the route with staggered platforms. *Norman Turnbull*

On 4 August 1990 only the platforms remain. However, the line of the former trackbed can easily be seen and one has the impression that it would be a simple task to replace the track and have trains running again in no time at all. One can only dream!

FALAHILL SUMMIT: 'Peak' No D13 at Falahill summit on 26 May 1962. The line was 800 feet above sea level at this point and southbound trains had a gruelling 9-mile climb, mostly at 1 in 90, in order to reach this spot. *Michael Mensing*

Today the location is almost unrecognisable as a former main line. The railway house (out of the picture to the left) remains as a private dwelling, but all other signs of the railway have gone. The trackbed is now populated with weeds and bushes growing through the ballast.

INNERLEITHEN: A view of the station, taken in about 1962, looking west from the tall signal box and clearly showing the staggered platforms. Innerleithen was on the Galashiels to Peebles line which followed the River Tweed and was opened on 18 June 1866. Passenger services ceased on 5 February 1962. *Norman Turnbull*

The station house has survived and on 4 August 1990 it was in the course of renovation as a private house. The platform immediately in front of the house together with the canopy have been retained, as has the small square building to the right of the house. The present picture is from a lower angle, as the tall signal box has long since gone, but the westbound platform remains, topped by a couple of demountable buildings. The large building on the right, however, has been demolished, the area now forming part of a sawmill.

CARDRONA: Class 'J37' 0-6-0 No 64577 works the daily pick-up goods from Peebles eastward across the River Tweed. The line was known as the 'Peebles Loop' as it left the Waverley Route at Galashiels, looped westward through Peebles then turned north to re-join the Waverley at Eskbank, near Dalkeith. The passenger service was withdrawn from the line on 5 February 1962. *Hugh Ballantyne*

Very little visual change has taken place at this location. The track, telegraph pole and signal are long gone, but the bridge remains as a footpath. Fifty yards to the east of this spot, the station survives almost complete, but is hidden from view by many bushes.

PEEBLES CR STATION: At one time Peebles boasted two stations, the North British to the north of the River Tweed and the Caledonian to the south. The two stations were linked by a single-track bridge over the river, but very little traffic used this link. A feature of Peebles was the running of meat trains direct to the London markets. *Hugh Ballantyne*

Today the station site is occupied by Tweedbridge Court, a home for the elderly and disabled, and the foreground area is a housing estate. Because of these developments an exact location photograph was not possible, but a picture was obtained from a roof garden at Tweedbridge Court. The bridge is the one seen in the background of the 'past' picture. The railway ran under this bridge and along an embankment for a couple of hundred yards before swinging left over the River Tweed to join the North British line. The rail bridge no longer exists, but the embankment is a popular picnic spot.

LEADBURN: The station as seen in 1962. The line from Eskbank to Peebles opened on 4 July 1855, then a line from Leadburn to Dolphinton in Lanarkshire was opened on 4 July 1864. This latter line left the Peebles loop at Leadburn Junction, half a mile south of Leadburn station. *Norman Turnbull*

On 4 August 1990 the platforms are still intact and the former trackbed is now in use as a picnic area. The house in the background, where the railway crossed the road, is still lived in, and the roof of the building just visible behind the bushes on the left is the Leadburn Inn, the restaurant of which is actually a maroon Mk 1 coach.

ROSEWELL & HAWTHORNDEN: A Gloucester RCW DMU set stands at Rosewell station in July 1962 on a train to Edinburgh. Half a mile to the south-west of the station was Hawthornden Junction where the Penicuik branch left the Peebles loop. The branch opened on 2 September 1872. *Norman Turnbull*

The remains of the station as seen on 17 July 1990. The platforms are intact although the edging stones have been replaced by brickwork. The trackbed is now a footpath to Auchendinny and Penicuik, but nature is obscuring any other traces of the railway. The cottage in the background is still inhabited.

AUCHENDINNY: The station as it looked in June 1965. Although the line opened on 2 September 1872, the passenger service only lasted until 10 September 1951. Nonetheless, the platform and track were in good order, although the buildings were showing signs of decay. The bridge in front of the short tunnel carried the track over the River North Esk. *Norman Turnbull*

Twenty-five years later and the station buildings have been replaced by trees and the trackbed is used as a footpath. As in many locations, the platforms have just been left to nature.

PENICUIK: The end of the 4-mile-long branch from Hawthornden Junction as seen in March 1967. The railway arrived in 1872 and finally closed on 27 March 1967, the passenger service having gone by 10 September 1951. A substantial amount of traffic was carried for mills in the town, but even they have now closed. *Norman Turnbull*

Apart from one small piece of the platform end, the whole of the railway has been swept away and the site left derelict to be returned to nature. This was the scene on 17 July 1990.

The Forth Bridge and East Fife

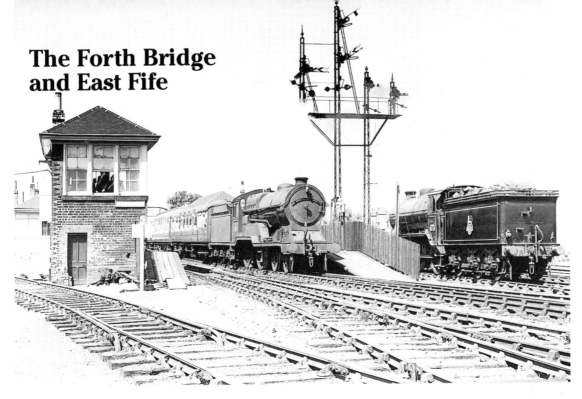

DALMENY (1): The station as seen on 16 July 1955 with 'D11/2' 4-4-0 No 62691 *Laird of Balmawhapple* about to depart with a Dunfermline to Edinburgh Waverley train, whilst a 'K2/1' 2-6-0 waits in an adjoining siding. Note the rather fine array of signals and the signal box. *David A. Anderson*

Being at the southern end of the Forth Bridge, Dalmeny always enjoyed a frequent service to Edinburgh and today is no different. On 2 April 1990 'Sprinter' set No 150262 works the 17.05 Kirkcaldy to Edinburgh service. The main changes are the removal of the semaphores, signal box and sidings; a large relay room stands on the site of the box and the old North British footbridge has been replaced by a more modern structure. The buildings on the down platform remain in almost original condition and the awning can just be seen in the present picture.

DALMENY (2): Class 'J37' 0-6-0 No 64559 of Parkhead (Glasgow) shed, code 65C, rolls off the Forth Bridge on 16 July 1955 with a Fife coast to Glasgow Queen Street passenger working formed of vintage North British coaching stock. *David A. Anderson*

The Forth Bridge was celebrating its centenary year in 1990. On 2 April a Class '101' Metro-Cammell unit approaches Dalmeny station working ECS to Haymarket Depot. Changes to the scene include the lengthening of the up platform, removal of the 'scissors' crossover and replacement of the semaphore signals by electric colour lights controlled by the power box at Edinburgh Waverley. The lines across the bridge are signalled for bi-directional running. As to the bridge itself – well, its appearance has not altered in a hundred years!

NORTH QUEENSFERRY: The tunnel mouth at the north end of the station on 24 August 1957 as 'B1' 4-6-0 No 61245 *Murray of Elibank* bursts out with a stopping train for Edinburgh Waverley. The south end of the station is but a few yards from the end of the Forth Bridge. *J.C. Beckett*

A similar scene on 2 April 1990 as 'Sprinter' 150283 enters the station on a stopping train to Edinburgh. The 'Sprinters' may not be as photogenic as a 'B1', but they have succeeded in revitalising local rail travel around Fife and to Edinburgh judging by the sharply increasing passenger figures.

INVERKEITHING (1): Looking north from the down platform of Inverkeithing station as 'J37' 0-6-0 No 64636 hurries past with a return Sunday School excursion from Anstruther to Glasgow Queen Street on 20 June 1959. Apart from the smartly turned out locomotive, it is worth noting the vintage stock, the fine array of signals, and the foreground notice and light to protect staff crossing the tracks. *David A. Anderson*

'Sprinter' 150264 at the same spot on 2 April 1990 with an 'Outer Circle' working which will form the 15.44 to Edinburgh Waverley. The signalling has been altered to colour lights, the bridge in the background has been rebuilt but the warning light and notice have been retained, albeit in a modernised form. The junction can just be seen under the bridge with the Dunfermline lines going to the left and the Kirkcaldy lines to the right. Trains arriving from the Kirkcaldy direction appear with little warning, hence the need for the protected crossing.

INVERKEITHING (2): The view as seen from the B981 road to Crossgates on 29 June 1957. 'J37' 0-6-0 No 64569 pulls away from Inverkeithing with an excursion to the Fife coast made up of eight suburban coaches. The line to Dunfermline can be seen in the background. These handsome Reid-designed locomotives were used for freight traffic but on summer Saturdays they were pressed into use for passenger workings and were frequent visitors to Fife. *David A. Anderson*

A Strathclyde Transport-liveried 'Sprinter' No 156511 at the same location on 3 April 1990 working the 08.45 from Edinburgh, whilst another 'Sprinter' stands on the Dunfermline line awaiting access to Inverkeithing station. Out of the picture to the right is a single line which completes the triangle between the Kirkcaldy and Dunfermline lines. The location has altered substantially over the years with the three tracks now reduced to two and the intrusion of vegetation on the left. There has been much house-building on the hilltop and a number of factories have sprung up in the background. Despite all this, the two trees on the right do not appear to have developed very much.

CLUNY: A once common scene in Fife as 'J38' 0-6-0 No 65914 heads for Thornton with a train of coal and scrap metal. The location is where the B922 road crosses over the Dunfermline to Thornton line about 4 miles west of Thornton. The 'J38' Class were regular performers in the area. *Roger Siviter*

Today the semaphore and the telegraph poles have gone, as also have the mill and chimney in the background. It is not all negative though, as 'Sprinter' No 150262 passes with an 'Outer Circle' working on 9 September 1989. To the end of the 1988/89 winter timetable, the local trains terminated at either Cardenden or Kirkcaldy, but from 15 May 1989 they continued round in a circle thus bringing passenger trains back to this section of the track. Trains running clockwise from Inverkeithing are 'Outer Circle', whilst anti-clockwise they are 'Inner Circle'. Despite all these changes it is refreshing to see that the platelayers' hut and the concrete ballast box have survived.

THORNTON MPD (62A): A view of the yard and coaling plant on 8 June 1957 with several ex-LNER classes in evidence including 'J88' 0-6-0T No 68331, 'D30' 4-4-0 No 62418 *The Pirate*, a 'J37' 0-6-0 and another 'D30'. At one time Thornton had an allocation of 113 locos, primarily for hauling coal trains from the numerous coalfields in Fife but also for working local passenger services. The shed finally closed in 1967. *Gavin W. Morrison*

What a transformation! All evidence of this once major depot has been swept away and the area returned to a green field site on which sheep graze. The only linking feature is the electricity pylon.

THORNTON WEST JUNCTION: 'B1' 4-6-0 No 61133 passes Thornton West Junction with a freight on 8 July 1965 and heads towards the MPD and the extensive marshalling yards. *Peter Skelton*

A fair number of changes have taken place over the years. The signal box, sidings and telegraph poles have gone whilst the building on the left has been replaced by a more modern structure. Even the street lighting has been updated. 'Sprinter' No 150255 passes by on 9 September 1989 on an 'Inner Circle' service. The introduction of 'Sprinters' on a frequent interval service has been rewarded with a large increase in passenger figures.

THORNTON JUNCTION STATION: On 28 March 1964, 'A2' 'Pacific' No 60527 *Sun Chariot* storms north out of the station with a Dundee train. The 'A2s' were no strangers to the area, and indeed Dundee (Tay Bridge) shed retained three of the class until the last days of steam in Scotland. *Rodney Lissenden*

It is hard to believe that this is the same location, as the large station has gone leaving Thornton with no station at all. Behind the 'Sprinter', working the 11.25 Edinburgh Waverley to Dundee service, can be seen the junction, with the main line to Kirkcaldy going out of the left of the picture whilst the single chord line to Thornton West Junction disappears to the right, behind the train. The house on the right is the only surviving feature.

THORNTON STATION SIGNAL BOX: This large signal box stood to the north of the station on the main line to Dundee. Note the fine array of signals to cover all the various shunting movements. 'WD' 2-8-0 No 90350 approaches the station on 8 July 1965 with a rake of suburban stock. Although they spent most of their time hauling coal trains, the 'WDs' were occasionally pressed into use on ECS or passenger services. No 90350 spent most of its life allocated to 62A, Thornton, a depot which had a sizeable allocation of this class. *Peter Skelton*

No longer a busy station throat, just a simple junction in the country, as 'Sprinter' 150208 runs past working the 11.52 Dundee to Edinburgh service on 9 September 1989. Gone are the signal boxes and the semaphores. The line diverging to the right behind the 'Sprinter' goes to Cameron Bridge and Methil.

CAMERON BRIDGE: A Class 'B1' 4-6-0 No 61307 of St Margarets shed departs from Cameron Bridge station with the 08.55 from Edinburgh Waverley. This line left the Kirkcaldy to Dundee line at Thornton Junction and ran across to the coast at Leven. There was a spur from Cameron Bridge to Lochty which opened in August 1888 and survived until 1964. Just over a mile of the line remains as the Lochty Private Railway, and was for a number of years the home of No 60009 *Union of South Africa*. *J.C. Beckett*

Time seems to have passed the station by as the platforms are totally intact, as is the North British lattice footbridge situated just out of view. The far line is the through line for Leven and Methil, whilst the near line is in fact a siding from the Scottish Grain Distillers plant in the background. Unlike most of the pictures, here the trees have been thinned out, revealing the house on the right.

ELIE: A typical rural scene as 'D11/2' 4-4-0 No 62677 *Edie Ochiltree* pulls out of Elie station with a train for Crail on 10 September 1958. The prestige train down this line was the 'Fife Coast Express'; in fact, it was two trains, one from Glasgow and one from Edinburgh, both terminating at Crail. The Edinburgh train even boasted a restaurant car for a short period. In the 1950s the Glasgow train used the former 'Silver Jubilee' coaches. On summer Saturdays, the line was often crammed with trains, but gradually traffic declined and the line was closed to passengers in September 1965. *J.C. Beckett*

On 11 March 1990 the decline of the railway can be seen to be complete. No trace exists, and the station and goods yard site is now a housing estate. Only a slight ridge across the field indicates the former route.

CRAIL: The station on 1 May 1965 with 'B1' 4-6-0 No 61330 about to depart with a train to Thornton Junction. The line closed in the following September. Crail was the terminus for the majority of trains using the coast route but for a time some trains from Edinburgh to Dundee also used this route. In addition there were some services which worked through to St Andrews. *W.A.C. Smith*

Nearly 25 years later, and what a transformation! The station building is in use as a private house, but unfortunately the extensions are of the modern box style and not at all in keeping with the original architecture. The platform edging can be found in the undergrowth, but the whole area is now rather untidy compared to the original scene.

COALTOWN OF BALGONIE: Just over a mile north of Thornton the line passes under the B9130 road in a deep cutting. Part of the village can be seen in the background. On 13 April 1963, Birmingham RCW Type 2 Bo-Bo No D5383 heads south with a short van train. *Rodney Lissenden*

On 9 September 1989, the 13.54 Dundee to Edinburgh service is worked by 'Sprinter' No 150248. The most obvious change over the years is the way in which the vegetation has taken over both sides of the cutting and now totally obscures the houses of the village. The other change is the dramatic fall-off in freight traffic in the area.

MARKINCH: 'B1' 4-6-0 No 61330 pulls away from Markinch with a van train for Edinburgh and passes the very attractive signal box. There were still semaphore signals around on 2 September 1966. *Les Nixon*

As in so many other pictures, the signal box, semaphores and telegraph poles are long gone. However, the concrete panel hut is still visible as 47701 *Saint Andrew* rushes through the station with the 12.10 Aberdeen to Edinburgh train on 9 September 1989. In fact, the signal box has been replaced by a large relay room some 30 yards to the south of this spot. On the extreme left can be seen the shed which was, until recently, home to No 60009 *Union of South Africa*. The branch which ran to Leslie is seen running out at the left of the picture, but now only extends a couple of miles to the Tullis Russel paper plant at Auchmuty.

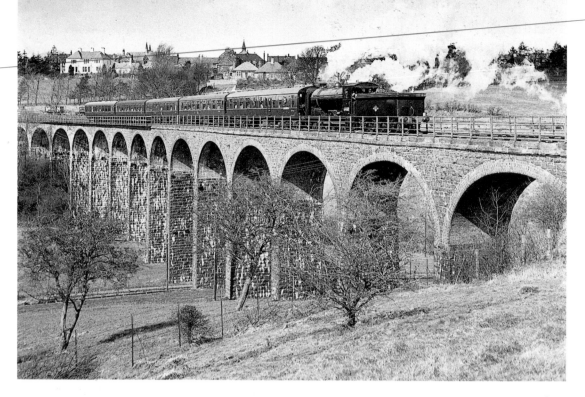

LESLIE (1): An immaculate 'J37' 0-6-0 No 64618 crosses Leslie viaduct with an SLS/BLS Easter special, returning to Markinch on 13 April 1963. *Rodney Lissenden*

The beautiful viaduct remains today and is used as a walkway, and whilst the bushes and trees have grown, very little else has changed – or so it would appear at first glance. On closer inspection, however, the building in the 'past' picture with the twin spires has now disappeared and some buildings, as part of Smith Anderson's paper mill, have been erected on the right.

LESLIE (2): 'J38' 0-6-0 No 65909 shunts the small yard at the end of the branch in August 1966. *Les Nixon*
On 9 September 1989 only the goods shed survives of all the former railway features. The most obvious change to the landscape is the absence of the large tree – not even a trace of the stump could be found!

LESLIE (3): A view of the small yard at Leslie in August 1966. 'J38' 0-6-0 No 65909 shunts a load of coal bound for the nearby Smith Anderson paper mill. The loading gauge and the ornate lamp bracket make this a real period scene. *Les Nixon*

As in so many locations, the railway has now been completely obliterated, and part of the site is now given over to modern housing.

NEAR LEUCHARS: 'A3' 'Pacific' No 60098 *Spion Kop* heads south towards Leuchars Junction on 14 August 1959, with an Aberdeen to Edinburgh express – note the different coach liveries. At Leuchars Junction, passengers could change for a train to St Andrews until the line closed to both passengers and freight on 6 January 1969. Leuchars was also where the Tayport Branch rejoined the main line. *J.C. Beckett*

The scene on 11 March 1990 shows the 13.30 Dundee to Edinburgh service now operated by 'Sprinters'. Very little has changed during the intervening years, but the house/garage above the dome of the 'A3' has been demolished and some modern bungalows have been erected. The background forest has grown and St Michael's golf course has a more manicured look. The gentleman approaching the green is evidently not interested in the present-day railway scene!

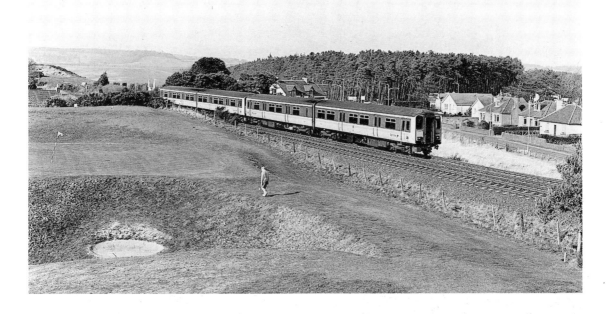

West Fife and Clackmannan

DUNFERMLINE MPD: A view of the rear of Dunfermline shed (62C) on 31 March 1961. The shed was a medium-sized depot with four roads and during steam days it had an allocation of around 70 locos. The shed building was re-roofed in the mid 1950s whilst a new coaling plant and turntable were brought into use in 1952. The bulk of the duties were freight turns and this was reflected in the allocation of loco types. In this view can be seen representatives of Classes 'Y9', 'N15', 'J88', 'WD' and 'J38'; note the wooden tender attached to the 'Y9' saddle tank. The shed was situated on the south side of the direct line from Cowdenbeath to Alloa and to the east of Dunfermline Upper station; it closed with the end of steam on the Scottish Region on 1 May 1967. *Noel A. Machell*

On 24 April 1990 there is no sign of the motive power depot, and the site is now used by Taggarts, an Austin-Rover dealer. The retaining wall in the right background of both pictures supported the main line to Dunfermline Upper and on to Alloa. Today the trackbed is used as a roadway and a parking area for Dunfermline Athletic Football Club.

DUNFERMLINE LOWER: Preserved NBR 4-4-0 No 256 *Glen Douglas* with a tour train west of Dunfermline Lower station on 30 March 1964. The line connected Dunfermline with Stirling via Kincardine and Alloa. The section from Alloa to Stirling closed to passengers on 7 October 1968. *Rodney Lissenden*

The same view on 24 April 1990, and the bridge and the gasholder still remain. The large building on the left-hand side, a bakery, has been demolished and the site is now an estate of luxury houses. The most surprising survivor of all is the corrugated iron hut at the trackside, which appears totally out of step with the modern surroundings. The line remains open for traffic to Crombie and Longannet and, if needed, to Kincardine also. For a line with very little traffic it is surprising to note that the track is laid with long welded rail on concrete sleepers. Most of the line through to Alloa and Stirling is intact and there are rumours of a possible re-opening to passenger traffic. Certainly there has been a huge increase in private housing in this area and there are plenty of commuters to Edinburgh who would, in all probability, support a train service.

KELTY JUNCTION: A picture full of industry with NBR 4-4-0 No 256 *Glen Douglas* having just arrived from Edinburgh with a railtour on 13 April 1963, and the background comprising a large colliery complete with its own loco shed in the centre of the picture. Just peeping out to the left behind the loco shed in the centre of this picture is a flat-roofed building which was the electricity sub-station. A large bridge spanned all the tracks at this point, from which the picture was taken. Kelty Junction was on the direct main line from the Forth Bridge to Perth via Glenfarg, but there were other lines to various collieries including one line which crossed through the centre of Loch Ore on a series of bridges and islands. Needless to say coal trains formed the main traffic. *Rodney Lissenden*

Well, is it the same place? It needed two visits by the photographer and a chat to the local farmer to confirm the exact spot. There have been significant changes here, not only to the railway but also to the topography. The colliery has been closed and removed completely including the spoil heap or 'byng' in the left background. The railway has been completely dismantled and the embankment bulldozed flat, returning the landscape to what it was before the railway came. The large bridge was also a casualty. With all these changes, did anything survive? The building in the centre of the field is the electricity sub-station mentioned above which has been refurbished and fitted with a pitched roof. The trees on the skyline are the same and the road running down behind the sub-station can still be seen. The area in the foreground is a car park for people visiting Lochore Meadows Country Park. A far cry from the previous use of the land!

MAWCARSE JUNCTION: This junction was where the line from Ladybank via Auchtermuchty joined the Perth via Bridge of Earn to Edinburgh line just south of Glenfarg; it was situated to the north of Loch Leven, 4 miles north of Kinross. On 13 April 1963, *Glen Douglas* comes off the Auchtermuchty line with an enthusiasts' special. The line from Bridge of Earn to Mawcarse opened in May 1890 and closed on 5 January 1970, whilst the line from Ladybank through Auchtermuchty closed on 5 October 1964, the passenger service having already been withdrawn many years before in June 1950. *Rodney Lissenden*

Apart from the removal of the track and the growth of the trees, very little has changed in this quiet part of Fife.

RUMBLING BRIDGE (1): *Glen Douglas* again, this time pulling away from the picturesque setting of Rumbling Bridge station in the Devon Valley on 13 April 1963. Note the magnificent tall home signal guarding the approaches to the station for eastbound trains. The line from Kinross to Rumbling Bridge was opened on 1 May 1863 and from Rumbling Bridge to Dollar on 1 May 1871. The line closed to both passengers and freight on 15 June 1964. *Rodney Lissenden*

The scene as recorded on 3 April 1990 retains only the large house on the hill, now partially obscured by trees. The remainder of the site is now covered by executive-style homes, and looking at the picture it is hard to believe that a railway once ran through this spot.

RUMBLING BRIDGE (2): A view from the signal box on 16 August 1959 as 'B1' 4-6-0 No 61244 *Strang Steel* and Stanier '5MT' 4-6-0 No 45492 run through Rumbling Bridge station with an up train diverted from the Gleneagles route. The Devon Valley Railway, as it was known originally, often played host to diversions when there was engineering work on the Stirling to Perth main line. *J.C. Beckett*

On 3 April 1990 the iron road is now a tarmac access road to a group of houses, but the westbound platform survives. The waiting room on the platform has been replaced by a builder's store and the road overbridge in the background has been infilled with earth to form an embankment. Thanks are due to the owners of the bungalow from where the 'present' picture was taken – they were intrigued to know that a different form of transport used their access road just over a quarter of a century ago.

DOLLAR VIADUCT: Class '5MTs' Nos 45467 and 44885 double-head an up fish train from Aberdeen over the viaduct on 15 August 1959. The direct line through Gleneagles was closed for engineering work this day causing trains to be diverted through the Devon Valley. *J. C. Beckett*

The pillars of the viaduct were still standing proud on the evening of 3 April 1990, the decking having been removed many years ago. The original structure was 390 feet long and was built on a gentle curve which added to its graceful appearance. The space between the two nearest pillars is now filled with various sheds and pens for farm animals and poultry. The sheep and her young offspring are keeping a wary eye on the photographer.

TILLICOULTRY VIADUCT: *Glen Douglas* again, with the tour train on 13 April 1963, making good progress across the viaduct with the mill town of Tillicoultry in the background. *Rodney Lissenden*

As at Dollar viaduct, the girder spans and decking have been removed leaving just the pillars. On the two central piers the reinforcing straps have also been removed for some reason. The background has also undergone some change, with not one mill chimney now in evidence and in some cases even the mill itself having been demolished. Even so it was a scene of tranquility on the spring evening of 3 April 1990. The Devon Valley line from Kinross in the east to Alloa in the west passed through some quite beautiful countryside in the shelter of the Ochil Hills.

ALLOA: The station on 2 September 1955 with Class 'D34' 4-4-0 No 62470 *Glen Roy* leaving with the 16.21 from Perth to Glasgow Queen Street. The line to Alloa opened on 28 August 1850 and the section to Stirling on 1 July 1852. Owing to an increase in traffic a new station was completed in 1888. *W.A.C. Smith*

The scene on 4 April 1990 shows that the wide open spaces of the former station have gone and in their place is the 'Leisure Bowl' recreation centre. The brewery on the right, for which Alloa is famous, has changed little over the years apart from a few minor improvements. It is encouraging to note, however, that whilst not in use meantime, a single track remains, and perhaps a service from Stirling to Dunfermline will be introduced in the not too distant future.

MENSTRIE: Class 'J36' 0-6-0 No 65323 heads past Menstrie with a tour train on the Alva branch on 13 April 1963. The mass of the Ochil Hills can be seen in the background. *Rodney Lissenden*

The Alva branch is still in use today but it only goes as far as the distillery at Menstrie which is just beyond the bridge. The traffic consists of molasses tanks which arrive at Stirling on a Speedlink service and are then tripped to Menstrie. On 6 April 1990, English Electric Type 1 locos Nos 20206 and 20213 depart from Menstrie Distillers with the return molasses tanks. From Stirling the train takes the Alloa line as far as Cambus; it then runs round in order to gain access to the branch at Alva Line Junction. The current scene shows the tremendous amount of growth by the trees and bushes; those on the left screen a large housing estate.

Stirling to Hilton Junction

STIRLING (1): Class '5' 4-6-0 No 45183 of Dalry Road shed (64C) stands at the head of the 10.15 to Edinburgh Princes Street in September 1964. Over the years, Stirling has been one of the cleanest stations in the Scottish Region, and it certainly appears so in this picture. *David A. Anderson*

The scene on 6 April 1990 shows a complete contrast in motive power with HST car No 43196 heading the Inverness to London King's Cross 'Highland Chieftain' service. The trackwork and station buildings are just as they were and just as tidy. Apart from the train, only the lamp standards and modern platform number sign are clues to the era.

STIRLING (2): 'Clan' 'Pacific' No 72007 *Clan Mackintosh* restarts an Aberdeen to Glasgow express past Stirling shed on 22 July 1964; it is 21.25 and the loco is catching the last rays of a setting sun. Evidence of the diesel age is visible in the shed together with a rather grubby 'Black Five'. The 'Clans' gave stalwart service on this route but they were not the most popular class of locos with the crews. Stirling South shed closed in June 1966 although some locos remained stored in and around the shed after this date. A fine signal gantry can be seen in the background. *Rodney Lissenden*

A closer view of the gantry, and 'A4' 'Pacific' No 60007 *Sir Nigel Gresley* accelerates away with an Aberdeen to Glasgow express on 22 August 1964. The 'A4s' became famous for working these trains in the last days of Scottish steam. In the shed road is North British Type 2 No D6110. It is interesting to note that the steam loco is still being used on main-line excursions today whilst the 'modern' diesel loco was withdrawn many years ago. *W.M.J. Jackson*

Stirling South today, and a line of bushes now occupy the position from where the original photograph was taken. Because of this, the picture on 4 April 1990 was taken from the road overbridge and depicts 'Super Sprinter' No 156445 leaving Stirling with the 17.32 Dunblane to Edinburgh service. The gasholder and, in the left background, Stirling Middle signal box survive, but the shed building has been demolished, although the trackwork, albeit somewhat overgrown, remains intact. What, presumably, were the shed offices are now small industrial units and offices.

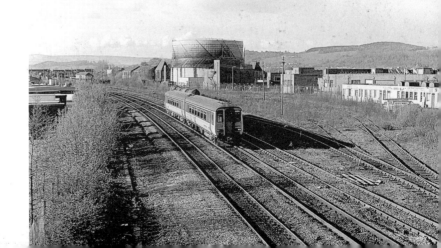

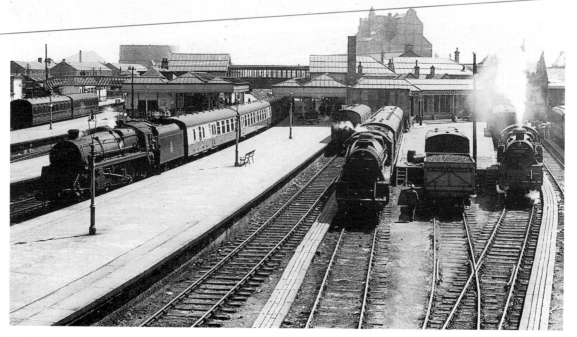

STIRLING (3): The north end of Stirling station on 8 June 1957. Standard class '5' No 73146, of St Rollox shed (65B), awaits the road with a Glasgow Buchanan Street to Dundee train, whilst on the right ex-LMS Class '5' No 45334 and local Standard 2-6-4T No 80125 await their next duties. *Gavin W. Morrison*

The same view on 4 April 1990 shows Brush Class '47/7' No 47717 *Tayside Region* leaving the platform with the 13.25 Glasgow to Aberdeen service. The large building in the background has gone but the rest of the architecture appears to be in a 'time warp'. The main change is from steam to diesel traction as evidenced by the oil tanks standing where the coal wagons used to be stabled. These pictures were taken from the road bridge which crosses right over the end of the station. To the north of this bridge, in steam days, was situated the other loco shed, Stirling Shore Road. This was the North British shed and served as a sub-shed to Stirling South shed until 1958.

BRIDGE OF ALLAN: Class 'A4' 4-6-2 No 60026 *Miles Beevor* coasts towards the station with an Aberdeen to Glasgow train on 3 July 1964. This was one of the famous 3-hour expresses which gave the 'A4s' a last chance to show their paces. The original station platforms ran under the bridge carrying the A9 road, but the station has been completely rebuilt to a site to the south of the road. *Rodney Lissenden*

A change of pace as a Strathclyde-liveried Derby-built DMU set No 107733 slows for the station on 4 April 1990 with the 14.43 Dunblane to Glasgow. As can be seen, the goods yard on the right-hand side has gone and the track layout much simplified. The site of the former goods yard is now occupied by a caravan sales company, the owner of which lives in the old station house which still retains its old character. The station enjoys an extremely frequent service from the Edinburgh to Dunblane and Glasgow to Dunblane services.

KINBUCK: A mixed freight climbs through the station on 28 May 1965 hauled by English Electric Type 1 No D8033. Kinbuck is the summit of a 5-mile climb from near Stirling at gradients ranging from 1 in 135 to 1 in 74. *Noel A. Machell*

Push-pull-fitted Class '47' No 47710 *Sir Walter Scott* heads north past the site of the station with the 15.25 Glasgow to Aberdeen train on 4 April 1990. The signals, platforms and telegraph poles are all gone, but the station building, now a private residence, survives. The wooden ballast box in the foreground is partially intact, but the roof of the barn in the background looks extremely tired!

GLENEAGLES (1): The approach to Gleneagles from the west is in a deep cutting and 'Britannia' 'Pacific' No 70035 *Rudyard Kipling* is seen here heading a freight on 2 July 1964. During the mid-60s, members of the class based at Carlisle Kingmoor depot were regular visitors to the area on passenger, parcels or freight turns. *Rodney Lissenden*

In this July 1989 scene there has been substantial change. The semaphores and lineside poles have gone, although new poles have been erected on the cutting top. The nearside slope of the cutting is a mass of rose-bay willow-herb as Class '47' No 47709 *The Lord Provost* approaches with the 11.25 Glasgow to Aberdeen express.

GLENEAGLES (2): Gleneagles was the junction for the branch to Crieff and on 2 July 1964 a Park Royal railbus No M79973 has just pulled out of the bay platform and is curving away from the main line. Even the introduction of these lightweight railbuses could not reduce costs sufficiently to save the line, and the branch closed four days later on 6 July. *Rodney Lissenden*

By 25 July 1989, all trace of the branch had gone apart from the immediate trackbed which is used as a short access road. Needless to say, the vegetation has taken over and the roof of the house on the right is only just visible. Meanwhile, Class '47' No 47597 passes by on the main line with the 11.42 Edinburgh to Inverness train.

CRIEFF: This beautiful town was at the end of the 8-mile branch from Gleneagles where it joined the Perth to Balquhidder line. The town is pictured on 17 July 1962 with the station and its distinctive platform awnings in the foreground. Crieff is situated in a very attractive part of Scotland and always attracts a large number of tourists. The Crieff Hydro is a particularly famous hotel. The station was always kept in an immaculate condition and it was very close to the town centre. The line from Perth was opened in May 1866, whilst the line to Crieff Junction (later renamed Gleneagles) had opened some ten years previously. The line was extended westwards to Comrie in July 1893, St Fillans in 1901, Lochearnhead in 1904 and finally to Balquhidder in 1905, thus forming a connection with the Callander & Oban line. The branch to Gleneagles closed in 1964 but the line to Perth managed to survive until 1967. *Ron Herbert*

The scene on 3 April 1990 presents a very sorry sight. The station was completely removed and the land lay derelict until an ambulance station and health centre were recently built. The rest of the town's features remain unchanged.

COMRIE: A typically rural scene, with no sense of urgency as Wickham railbus No 79967 arrives at the station on 17 July 1962 with the 18.05 service from Gleneagles. With only a population of around 2,000 there was never going to be a large amount of passenger traffic, but even the introduction of the railbuses could not stop the inevitable and the line closed on 6 July 1964. *Ron Herbert*

In the contemporary scene the station has gone to be replaced by the 'Riverside Caravan Park'. The only linking feature is the wall in the bottom right-hand corner.

AUCHTERARDER (1): Class '5' No 44975 approaches Auchterarder from the south-west with a stopping train to Perth on 30 July 1964. The Class '5s' were no strangers to this former Caledonian Railway route and they continued to dominate local passenger and freight turns right to the end of steam. *Rodney Lissenden*

Class '47' No 47604 *Women's Royal Voluntary Service* working the 13.33 Glasgow to Inverness service on 25 July 1989. There has been surprisingly little change to the scene. The point rodding has been moved to the outside of the siding and the up main starter has been re-sited nearer to Gleneagles and is no longer visible from this angle. It is pleasing to see that the small lattice post semaphore controlling the siding still remains.

AUCHTERARDER (2): Looking to the north-east, 'A4' 'Pacific' No 60027 *Merlin* passes Auchterarder signal box with an Aberdeen to Glasgow 3-hour express on 30 July 1964. Many excellent runs were recorded on these trains as the crews showed what could be achieved in the dying years of steam. *Rodney Lissenden*

In comparison Class '47' No 47452 *Aycliffe* heads south with an Inverness to London Euston train on 25 July 1989. Today the station has gone and with it the station buildings, which can just be seen above the second coach in the 'past' picture. The crane on the loading dock has gone but the loading platform is retained and the down sidings are used occasionally by permanent way department wagons. The goods yard site is still used by a coal merchant, but the coal no longer arrives by rail. The up siding in the foreground has not seen a train on it in a long time. The signal box is altered to the extent that a toilet has been added to the west wall. Finally the down home signal has been replaced by a more modern semaphore.

HILTON JUNCTION: This is the spot where the North British line joins the Caledonian line. On 20 June 1966, Peppercorn 'A2' No 60532 *Blue Peter* swings on to the Caledonian line with the 13.30 Aberdeen to Glasgow. Perth is 2 miles north of the junction, beyond the tunnel. This area was a favourite haunt of one of Scotland's best-known railway photographers, the late W.J.V. Anderson. *Roger Siviter*

Only the minimum of change has taken place here as 47595 *Confederation of British Industry* heads for Glasgow with the 12.30 from Inverness on 24 April 1990. Apart from the traction, the signalling location cabinets and the removal of the point rodding, the scene remains very much as it always was. Fortunately 60532 has been saved and is being restored to main-line standards by the North Eastern Locomotive Preservation Group with a view to a return to steam in 1991. It would be nice to be able to recreate the 'past' scene once more.

West Lothian

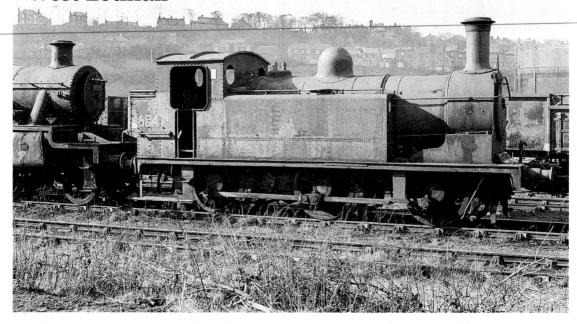

BO'NESS: In the latter days of steam, the extensive sidings at Bo'ness were used to hold condemned locos before being dispatched to meet their fate with a cutting torch. It became something of a Mecca for enthusiasts coming to pay their last respects. In that condition on 14 April 1963 can be seen 'J83' 0-6-0T No 68479 together with Stanier '3MT' 2-6-2T No 40200. The 4-mile long branch from Manuel, on the Edinburgh to Glasgow main line, to Bo'ness closed to passengers on 7 May 1956. *Rodney Lissenden*

Unlike many places, the old railway at Bo'ness is now expanding as it is the running line of the Scottish Railway Preservation Society who have made Bo'ness their headquarters. In the view on 15 July 1990 the new, brick-built loco shed can be seen on the right. The rather untidy area in the foreground is being used to store sleepers but eventually it will be returned to sidings in order to house the Society's extensive collection of wagons and coaches. The branch was recently re-connected to the main line, thus enabling easier movement of locomotives and coaches.

POLMONT: The station on 5 May 1956. On the right 'V2' 2-6-2 No 60964 *The Durham Light Infantry* arrives with the 18.00 Edinburgh Waverley to Glasgow Queen Street service, whilst on the left Ivatt Class '4' 2-6-0 No 43141 waits in the bay platform with the last train of the day to Bo'ness. The Bo'ness branch closed to passengers two days later, having originally opened in 1899 when on 1 February of that year the Caledonian Railway introduced a service from Glasgow Buchanan Street to Bo'ness. *W.A.C. Smith*

The down 'Clansman' rushes through Polmont station on 18 July 1990 with a Class '47/7' at its head. The Bo'ness bay platform has been filled in and the inevitable foliage has sprung up during the intervening years. The up platform has been shortened but the station retains a tidy and well-kept appearance.

BATHGATE (1): NBR 4-4-0 No 256 *Glen Douglas* makes a further appearance, heading east out of Bathgate Upper station on 25 March 1964. The railway reached Bathgate on 12 November 1849 as a branch from the Edinburgh to Glasgow main line at Ratho. On 11 August 1862 the line was extended west of Bathgate to Coatbridge, then a further extension was added taking services to Glasgow on 1 April 1871. A through service was introduced from Edinburgh to Glasgow (College) and this became a secondary, and somewhat slower, route. The line soon built up substantial mineral traffic, however, which became the major part of the line's revenue. The passenger service on the Bathgate route was withdrawn on 8 January 1956 but was reintroduced in 1986. Passenger figures on the new Bathgate to Edinburgh service have exceeded all expectations. *Rodney Lissenden*

The scene on 6 April 1990 shows substantial changes. What was the station approach is now the Bathgate Car Terminal where trainloads of brand new cars are unloaded and stored prior to distribution to dealerships. Bathgate station now has a new site and the platform can just be seen to the right behind the wire mesh fence. The original station was to the left.

BATGATE (2): 'J36' 0-6-0 No 65267 shunts at Bathgate Upper station on 30 March 1964. Coal traffic formed a major part of the revenue-earning services on the line for many years and the mineral wealth of the surrounding area contributed greatly to the fortunes of the railway companies. The 'J36' Class were common to the area and at one time Bathgate shed has no fewer than 25 of these locomotives on it books. *Rodney Lissenden*

The platform of Bathgate Upper station was still in evidence on 6 April 1990, on the left of the picture. The reception sidings for the car trains are on the right.

BATHGATE MPD: 'B1' 4-6-0 No 61344 rests at Bathgate shed (64F) on 29 March 1964. The photographer's car, a Ford Classic, admirably fills the rest of the picture. The shed originally had six roads but because of subsidence it was rebuilt in 1954 as a four-road shed. Over the years the bulk of locomotives allocated were 0-6-0s with Class 'J36' predominating. Fortunately, one of the class, No 65243 *Maude*, has been preserved and is currently undergoing restoration by the Scottish Railway Preservation Society at Bo'ness. Towards the end of steam, long lines of stored locomotives congregated at Bathgate, including some ex-LNER 'Pacifics'. *Rodney Lissenden*

Surprisingly the shed building was still standing on 6 April 1990 and was in use as a depot for repairing commercial vehicles. The old buildings on the right are relatively unchanged. The current photographer also parked in the same spot in the hope that some track and a 'B1' might reappear, but without success . . .

ARMADALE: No 256 *Glen Douglas* again at the head of the tour train as it passes through Armadale station heading towards Bathgate. Armadale was situated to the west of Bathgate on the NBR line to Coatbridge and Glasgow, which saw a great deal of mineral traffic in its boom years. This quickly declined after the Second World War and nowadays road transport moves coal from the few remaining workings in the area. *Rodney Lissenden*

When visited on 6 April 1990, it was a sorry sight with almost all trace of the railway gone. The trackside ballast box still rests proudly in its place, but the sleeper fence at the top of the cutting is somewhat the worse for wear. Beyond the fence the field gate is still in good order, although the general untidiness of the picture is typical of so many ex-railway sites today.

Edinburgh

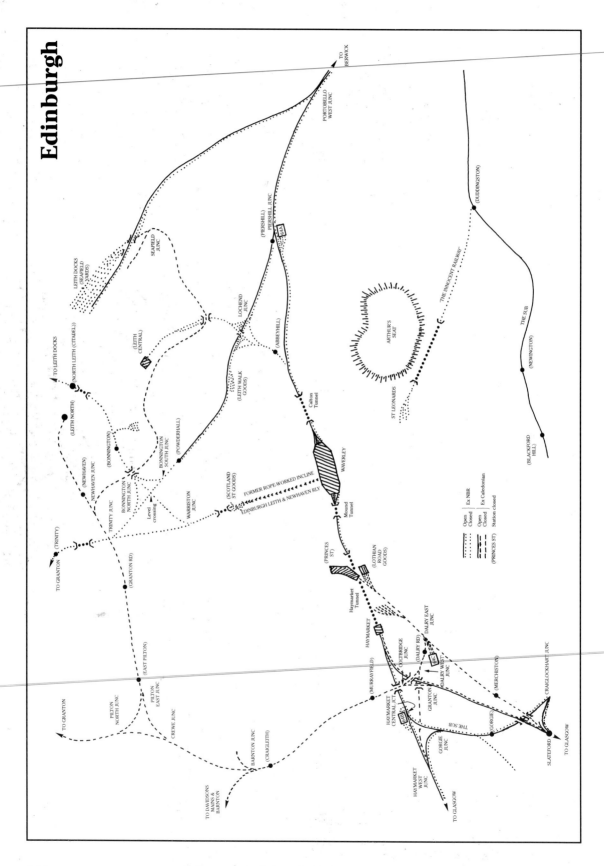

ST MARGARETS MPD (1): A view of the shed looking west in 1966. St Margarets was the senior shed in Edinburgh and was coded 64A. In this picture the shed roof is showing signs of neglect and there is a distinctly run-down atmosphere. The coaling plant is on the left of the picture but rather strangely there is no queue of locomotives waiting to take coal. Moreover, the air over the shed is relatively clean, which was most untypical. Because of the fumes generated by the depot, the adjacent road was known locally as 'Smokey Brae'. The shed lost most of its allocation in 1966 although it did not close until April 1967. Amongst the locomotives visible in the picture are Fairburn 2-6-4T No 42128, 'V2' 2-6-2 No 60869 and Standard Class '2' 2-6-0 No 78049. *Les Nixon*

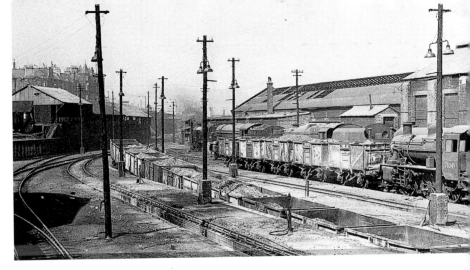

A somewhat different scene presented itself on 20 May 1990. The whole of the large depot has been flattened and two large office blocks erected on the site. The view is of St Margarets House and was taken from the access bridge to a similar building called Meadowbank House. Only the old tenement buildings on the left remain as a common link between the two pictures.

The plaque which marks the site of the well from which the area took its name.

THIS STONE MARKS THE SITE OF

ST MARGARET'S WELL

THE DRESSED STONEWORK OF THE FIFTEENTH-CENTURY WELLHOUSE BUILT OVER THIS ANCIENT MEDICINAL WELL AND CENTRE OF PILGRIMAGE WAS REMOVED IN 1859 AND USED TO BUILD A REPLICA OF IT OVER ST. DAVID'S WELL IN THE QUEEN'S PARK: AND THE OTHER REMAINS OF THE MEDIEVAL BUILDING WERE FILLED IN IN 1969

ST MARGARETS MPD (2): The turntable at the shed was tucked away in a corner and 'A4' 'Pacific' No 60001 *Sir Ronald Matthews* is being turned ready for its next duty. The shed closed in April 1967 when its last loco, No 65234, was finally sent for scrap. At one time St Margarets had the largest allocation in Scotland, over 220, but it was only in its last few years that it had its own allocation of 'Pacifics', namely 'A3s' and 'A4s', and then only in small numbers. It was the principal freight shed in the Edinburgh area and also one of the filthiest locations in the Scottish Region, not helped by being set low down with tenements overlooking two sides. *Bob Anderson*

The tenements remain, but the turntable area is now part of the car park beneath Meadowbank House.

WAVERLEY STATION (1): At the east end of the station, 'Peak' diesel No D13 awaits departure time with the 14.36 to Carlisle on 26 May 1962. The imposing building seen above the train is the former Calton Gaol. *Michael Mensing*
    On 25 April 1990, Class '08' No 08718 is stabled next to a Motorail van in the bay which was formerly platform 8. Platform 10 has been extended (on the right) and the 25Kv AC electrification wires are now in place. Calton tunnels can be seen in the background. It is not only the motive power that has changed over the years, as comparison of the luggage trolleys shows.

WAVERLEY STATION (2): The classic view from Regent Road of the east end of the station as 'V3' 2-6-2T No 67606 removes the empty stock of an arrival from King's Cross on 22 May 1962. Lots of diamond crossings, some with single slips, can be seen, as well as activity in the goods yards on the left. Plenty to look at and savour.
Michael Mensing

A complete transformation of the railway scene has taken place, and on 25 April 1990 the much simplified trackwork can be seen. There is now only one track through each of the two Calton Tunnels and not a single diamond crossing in sight, much to the relief of the S&T Department no doubt. The goods yard has been turned into a car park, and the signal box (above the second coach in the 'past' picture) has gone and been replaced by the large power box located at the far end of the car park. The extension of platform 10 beyond the overall roof can be seen, whilst platforms 2 and 3 on the right-hand side have been infilled. The current motive power in the form of an HST sits in platform 7 waiting to work the 11.00 service to London King's Cross. The overhead wires are in place and in the following year electric traction is scheduled to take over. Despite all these modernisations, steam has made a temporary comeback at Waverley in recent years, with the Scottish Railway Preservation Society organising 'Santa Specials' around the Suburban circle line and using a variety of steam locos in the process. The famous Edinburgh skyline, with the Castle on the rock, remains unchanged.

WAVERLEY STATION (3): The east end of Waverley in this third view, also taken on 22 May 1962, sees 'A3' 'Pacific' No 60078 *Night Hawk* approaching with an empty stock train. The extensive goods yard and, at the end of the train, the signal box are significant features. The 'A3' is fitted with a double chimney and trough smoke deflectors. *Michael Mensing*

On 25 April 1990, Class '47' No 47593 *Galloway Princess* also runs in with empty stock from Craigentinny Carriage Depot, to form the 11.42 to Inverness. As already remarked, the goods yard is now a large car park, the signal box is also long gone, the platform has been extended and the overhead wires are now in place.

WAVERLEY STATION (4): A once familiar scene at the west end of the station with the North British Hotel on the skyline. On 6 May 1957, 'V3' 2-6-2T No 67620 simmers at the head of empty stock, whilst 'B1' 4-6-0 No 61197 from Eastfield shed waits for parcels to be loaded before working the 10.40 to Dundee. The western end was used for departures to Glasgow, Fife, Dundee and Aberdeen, and was invariably busier than the eastern end. *Hugh Ballantyne*

The same view on 25 April 1990, as 'Sprinter' unit No 150259 runs into platform 15 with a train from Bathgate. Alongside in platform 14 a push-pull set waits to depart for Glasgow. This picture is already history as the Glasgow services are no longer worked by push-pull sets; instead, Class '156' 'Sprinters' are deputising pending the introduction of the '158' 'Express' units. In the background, the North British Hotel is shrouded in scaffolding as part of a full refurbishment and is due to re-open later in 1990. The clock was stopped at the time the picture was taken, but when working it is traditionally 2 minutes fast, to give travellers vital extra seconds when rushing for a train!

PRINCES STREET GARDENS: Surely one of the most photographed locations in the land, the gardens lie to the west of the station and provide a beautiful setting for trains entering and leaving Waverley station. On 19 June 1966 a Class '40' arrives from Aberdeen. The four tracks are extremely busy with intensive local services as well as destinations further afield. The imposing building in the background is the Caledonian Hotel behind which Princes Street station used to be located. Beyond the rear of the train is Haymarket Tunnel; the North British lines in the tunnel passed under the platform ends of the Caledonian Railway's Princes Street station. *Roger Siviter*

'Sprinter' unit 150284 runs through the gardens with an arrival from Dundee on 17 June 1990. Notice how the vegetation has extended, right over the track in some places. However, with the electrification being extended through the gardens on its way to Carstairs, much of the growth is being cut back. The most obvious changes are to the track layout, where double-track junctions with diamond crossings have been replaced with a series of 'ladder' crossings which are much cheaper to maintain.

HAYMARKET: 'A1' 4-6-2 No 60152 *Holyrood* eases off Haymarket shed (64B) near Haymarket Central Junction, and prepares to run backwards to Waverley Station on 8 September 1957. From there it worked a train to Aberdeen. The access tracks to the shed are on the left of the picture; the line running over the top is the Caledonian branch to Granton and Leith. *David A. Anderson*

The Caledonian line has long since been removed, but the embankment can still be seen. Regrettably all the 'A1s' were scrapped and the current scene on 27 April 1990 shows 'Sprinter' No 150284 on an Edinburgh to Dundee service.

ST LEONARDS BRANCH: 'J35' 0-6-0 No 64535 of St Margarets shed heads a short goods train towards St Leonards on a summer's evening in 1956. The line was opened on 4 July 1831 as the Edinburgh & Dalkeith Railway to bring coal to Edinburgh. It was known as 'The Innocent Railway' as it was initially operated as a horse-drawn railway, steam engines being thought dangerous. The branch to St Leonards skirted the south side of Arthur's Seat, the volcanic outcrop near the centre of Edinburgh, except for the last couple of hundred yards where it actually tunnelled through the rock. The tunnel mouth is just behind the photographer. *David A. Anderson*

The trackbed of the railway from St Leonards to Duddingston is now in use as a walkway and cycle track; the tunnel also remains and now has electric lighting. The large rock in the foreground has not weathered much in the 34 years to 28 May 1990!

Cast sign at the Duddingston end of the trackbed.

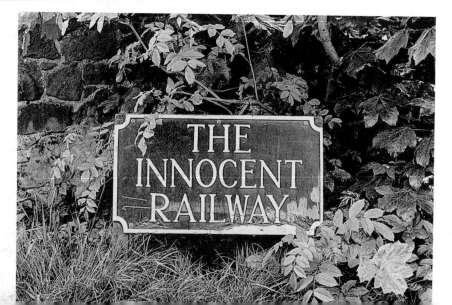

PRINCES STREET: A view of Princes Street station just a few days before it closed completely on 6 September 1965. A Stanier Class '5' 4-6-0 waits to depart on a train to Carstairs, while the Hillman Minx on the platform depicts the style of cars of the era. At one time over 60 suburban services departed from Princes Street each day in addition to the expresses to the south. Railway enthusiasts still remember the visits of the Welsh rugby team to Edinburgh in the '50s and '60s; as early as the Wednesday before the match the first excursion train would arrive and the numbers would increase until the Friday when a host of specials would converge on the Scottish capital.
David Easton

What a sad sight on 17 June 1990! No longer is there a main-line station served by four tracks. Instead the trackbed is now the Western Approach Road, and the platform area a car park – road has taken over from rail with a vengeance. The background buildings remain unchanged.

DALRY ROAD: Two Carlisle Kingmoor Class '5s' Nos 44676 and 44993 reverse out of Dalry Road shed (64C) to run down to Princes Street station on 22 June 1960. They are in pristine condition as their duty is the working of the Royal Train from Edinburgh to Euston via Carlisle. *David A. Anderson*

The tracks leading out of Dalry Road shed are now an access road to the Western Approach Road. The brewery in the background has been largely rebuilt over the years and about the only common feature is the flat-roofed building immediately above the firebox of the rear loco which is the same building beyond the middle vehicle in the picture taken on 28 May 1990.

MERCHISTON: Class 'D30' 4-4-0 No 62419 *Meg Dodds* with a train of vans heads towards Slateford, having passed through Merchiston station, which can just be seen beyond the bridge. This was part of the Caledonian line from Midcalder Junction to Princes Street. After the section from Slateford to Princes Street closed to traffic, trains travelled from Slateford along the Granton and Leith line as far as Granton Junction, but then they swung right to join up with the North British line at Haymarket and ran into Waverley. *David A. Anderson*

By 27 April 1990 there had been surprisingly little change. The former trackbed is now a tarmac access road to the Slateford Civil Engineers Depot. The houses remain as they were.

COLINTON: The station on the Caledonian Railway's branch to Balerno as seen in January 1966; the station buildings are boarded up and already showing signs of decay. The branch was in reality a loop, leaving the main line at Balerno Junction near Slateford and rejoining it at Ravelrig Junction near Balerno itself. The line attracted a good deal of traffic in the summer months and was very popular with the people of Edinburgh who wished to have a day in the country. It opened on 1 August 1874 but closed to passenger traffic on 30 October 1943, closing completely on 4 December 1967. *Norman Turnbull*

Totally unrecognisable as a former railway apart from the tunnel in the background, it is now a pleasant walk cum nature trail. Its origins are not forgotten, however, as a cast plaque on a stone cairn indicates that Colinton station opened on 31 October 1981 – unfortunately it was the nature trail which opened that day!

LEITH NORTH BRANCH: Branch lines as many people remember them. Caley 0-4-4T No 55202 and four suburban coaches work an afternoon train from Leith North to Edinburgh Princes Street on 17 May 1955, pictured at Ravelston, between Craigleith and Murrayfield. The Caledonian Railway opened the branch to passengers on 1 August 1879 and the service survived until 30 April 1962. The line served stations at Murrayfield, Craigleith, East Pilton, Granton Road and Newhaven before terminating at Leith North. *David A. Anderson*

On 27 April 1990 all trace of the railway has gone. Like many former lines around Edinburgh, it is now a walkway and cycle track complete with street lighting. Little else has changed, however, apart from the usual growth of vegetation.

Leith

LEITH NORTH: This view of the station on 21 May 1955 is so typical of the Edinburgh area at the time. Macintosh Caledonian '3F' 0-6-0 No 57559 stands at the head of the 12.05 departure for Edinburgh Princes Street. There is so much to savour in this picture – the tram car, the tenements, the lamp standard and the intricate detail in the end of the platform seat. The branch closed to passenger traffic on 30 April 1962, and the Caledonian Railway's terminus in Leith was no more. *W.A.C. Smith*

A much changed scene on 25 April 1990. Gone are the tenements and other trappings of the Victorian era, but surprisingly the train shed still survives and is in use by a marquee hire company. In the bottom left foreground can be seen part of the platform edging. The platform still exists but for the most part it is hidden under all the debris.

LEITH CENTRAL: This imposing structure was the North British Railway's main station in Leith and when the line closed to passengers on 7 April 1952 the building was used as a DMU maintenance depot. This was the scene on 2 October 1966. Even when its use as a maintenance depot ceased, the building remained as a landmark in the centre of Leith for many years. *Noel A. Machell*

The building was eventually demolished in early 1990 and the picture taken on 25 April shows the contractors in the final stages of tidying up the site. The track level was actually some 15 feet above the ground level shown, at the point where the dressed stonework starts.

NORTH LEITH: This was another North British station but, to avoid confusion with the Caley's Leith North station, this one was usually referred to as Leith Citadel. The station itself was to the right of this picture, taken on 19 November 1966. The lines actually continued over Commercial Street and entered the docks, passing between the large gateposts in the right background of the picture. The railway arrived in May 1846 and passenger services continued up to 16 June 1947. *David Easton*

The area has seen much redevelopment, and on 27 April 1990 only the retaining wall on the left remains to confirm that it is the same location. The goods yard is now a housing estate and just beyond the retaining wall, but out of the picture, is a large block of flats named Citadel Court – so the name lives on.

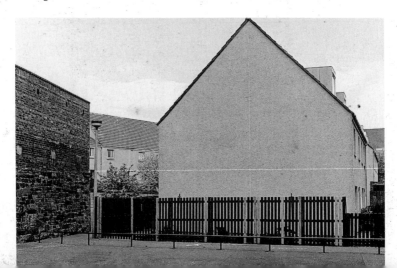

BONNINGTON STATION: The station as it appeared on a rather murky 19 November 1966 looking north-east towards Leith Citadel. The line opened on 10 May 1846, losing its passenger service in 1947, which would account for the run-down state of the station. *David Easton*

The view on 20 May 1990 is much more pleasing. The trackbed, like so many stretches of former railway around Edinburgh, has been turned into a pathway. The walls, bridges and platforms remain as built, but for once the foliage enhances the scene.

BONNINGTON SOUTH JUNCTION: Looking south-east on 19 November 1966, the line coming towards the camera ran to Trinity and Granton, whilst the line going to the left ran to Bonnington and Leith Citadel. Beyond the signal box is Powderhall station and the route to either Waverley or to Piershill Junction on the East Coast Main Line. Passenger traffic commenced on 22 March 1868. The mass of Arthur's Seat can be seen in the background. *David Easton*

As the bridge from which the 'past' picture was taken had been demolished, the picture on 28 May 1990 was taken from a lower angle. The line to Granton survived into the 1980s, albeit disused, and it has not long been lifted as can be seen from the ballast in the foreground. A plan to transport refuse by rail from the Powderhall Refuse Plant, which stands on the site of the old station, allowed the line from Piershill Junction to be reopened in 1989. The row of floodlights in the centre of the picture indicates the end of the branch. The refuse is carried in containers to Kaimes landfill site in West Lothian.

SCOTLAND STREET: The route north from Scotland Street Goods Depot was through a short tunnel under Broughton Road, as can be seen in this 1966 view. The once common 16-ton steel mineral wagon stands in front of the goods shed but there is a very run-down feel to the place. Once upon a time, this was the station for Granton Harbour and the ferry across to Burntisland in Fife. The line from Scotland Street to Trinity opened on 31 August 1842, with the section from Trinity to Granton opening on 19 February 1846. After closure to passengers the station remained as a goods depot. *David Easton*

The former station and goods yard on the edge of Edinburgh's New Town is now a rather attractive children's playground called 'Scotland Yard'. The large school building on the right remains unchanged but the large building in the centre, a cinema, has been demolished, revealing the junction of Broughton Road and Canonmills.

WARRISTON JUNCTION: Looking south on 19 November 1966, the right-hand line was the Granton to Scotland Street Goods line whilst the line entering from the left came from Leith Citadel and Bonnington. The section from the signal down to Scotland Street was presumably taken as a single yard as the sign on the signal post states that 'YARD WORKING BEGINS'. The small signal box is just by the bridge where the line crossed over the Water of Leith. *David Easton*

By 20 May 1990 all trace of the railway had gone and the trackbed was being used as a pathway. The garage and wooden fence remain but just look how nature has taken over! On the skyline can be seen the top of a monument which is lost in the haze of the 'past' picture; it stands, in fact, in St Andrew Square in the centre of Edinburgh, just 1 mile away.

TRINITY: The station as it appeared in May 1969, a couple of years after the branch closed. The North British reached Trinity on 31 August 1842 and extended to Granton on 19 February 1846. The Caledonian did not reach Granton until August 1861. The Trinity line closed in 1967 but the line as far as Powderhall remains in use today. *Norman Turnbull*

By 19 July 1990 the platforms had become heavily overgrown but were totally intact. The station house is now occupied as flats, as can be seen from the washing line. The roof of a more modern block of flats can be seen beyond the station roof.

INDEX OF LOCATIONS

Up-side sign on the East Coast Main Line.